SHE
Who BUILDS

90 Days of Purposeful Discipline

THIS PLANNER BELONGS TO

_____

_____

Title: She Who Builds: 90 Days of Purposeful Discipline
Author: Dr. Dashia

She's on Purpose Publishing
1659 HWY 20 W, #338
McDonough, GA 30253
United States

ISBN: 979-8-9989265-0-1

This is a work of non-fiction. The information contained within is based on the author's experiences and opinions. The author has made every effort to ensure the accuracy of the information within this book. However, the information provided herein is provided "as is" and the author and publisher disclaim any liability for any damages or losses that may result from the use of information contained within.

For more information, visit www.drdashia.com.

Printed in The United States

The Blueprint Begins

Welcome to She Who Builds:

90 DAYS OF PURPOSEFUL DISCIPLINE

This is more than a planner — it's your blueprint for intentional living.

Inside these pages, you'll find structure that meets your soul. Instead of chasing unrealistic to-do lists, you'll build your goals brick by brick, with purpose at the center. Whether you're

rebuilding, rising, or refining your next level — this 90-day journey is designed to help you align your time with your truth.

You'll gain clarity, track your growth, and stay focused without losing yourself in the grind. This planner breaks big dreams into powerful, daily actions — because consistency creates legacy.

Want help using this tool intentionally? **Take the 90-Day Builder's Training** at www.drdashia.com

Stay connected with the community:

Instagram and Facebook: @drdashia

YouTube: @shesonpurpose

Dear Queen,

Welcome.

Take a breath. You've just stepped into a sacred space — one created with you in mind.

She Who Builds isn't just about planning your days or checking boxes. It's about reclaiming your time, redefining what discipline looks like, and rising into the version of you that's been calling your name in the quiet moments.

This is for the woman who's tired of grinding and ready to grow.

The woman who knows she's chosen to build — her life, her legacy, her healing, her wealth, her faith.

Each page of this planner is a divine invitation to live on purpose. Not perfection. Not pressure. But purposeful discipline — the kind that aligns your goals with your soul, your schedule with your spirit, and your work with your why.

You'll be challenged. You'll be stretched. You'll be reminded of your brilliance.

And as you move through these 90 days, I pray you walk away more rooted in who you are and what you came here to do.

So take your pen.
Map out your mission.
And let's build.

With grace, power, and purpose,
Dr. Dashia
Founder, She's On Purpose
Curator of She Who Builds

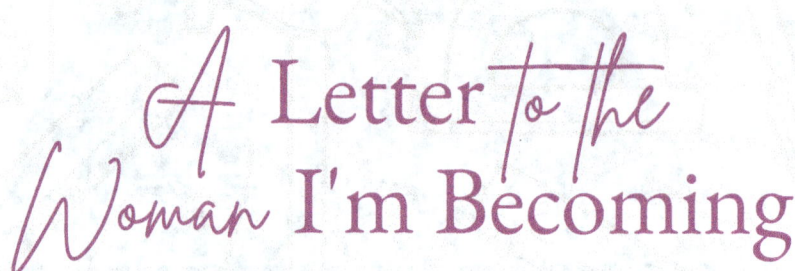

A Letter to the Woman I'm Becoming

Today, I commit to myself and my 90-day plan.
Use the space below to write a letter to the you 90 days from now.
What do you want that version of you to know?

_____

_____

_____

_____

_____

_____

_____

_____

_____

Foundation & Focus

Use this section to cast your vision and clarify your top 3 intentions for the season.
This is your why — the foundation you'll build on.

Visualize what success looks like.
Write it. Draw it. Paste images. Declare it.
Then, list the 3 goals that will anchor your next 90 days in purpose and power.

Top 3 *Goals* for the year

Goal: _____

Goal: _____

Goal: _____

My Alignment Audit

Use the chart below to rate where you are and where you want to be in each area of your life on a scale of 0–10. (0 = not present at all, 10 = fully aligned)

Subtract the two numbers to find your deficit — the gap between where you are and where you desire to be.

Then, circle your top 3 deficit areas — these are the zones to rebuild, refine, or renew over the next 90 days.

CATEGORY	WHERE I AM 👣	WANT TO BE 🌱	DEFICIT 📈
Health			
Money			
Personal Development			
Fun/Me Time			
Partner/ Relationship			
Career/ Business			
Friends/ Family			
Physical Environment			

Build *This* Quarter

Start with your top **3 goals** for this quarter — goals that align with your purpose and the areas you're ready to strengthen.

Then, break each goal into clear, aligned action steps that you can begin building over the next 90 days.

Think strategy meets soul — this isn't about hustle, it's about **intentional moves** that matter.

☀️ Goal 1:

☀️ Goal 2:

☀️ Goal 3:

Action Steps 📋

Action Steps 📋

Action Steps 📋

_____

_____

_____

WHY THIS GOAL MATTERS

Think positive.

Don't *forget* to smile.

Be kind to *yourself*.

It's ok to take a break.

Enjoy the *little* things.

_____

MAIN FOCUS

ACTUAL GOALS

_____

_____

_____

"One step at a
time. You'l get
there."

3 WAYS TO ACHIEVE MY GOALS

Add Month

_____

Notes	SUNDAY	MONDAY	TUESDAY
	☐	☐	☐
	☐	☐	☐
	☐	☐	☐
	☐	☐	☐
	☐	☐	☐

Add Year

_____

WEDNESDAY	THURSDAY	FRIDAY	SATURDAY
☐	☐	☐	☐
☐	☐	☐	☐
☐	☐	☐	☐
☐	☐	☐	☐
☐	☐	☐	☐

Weekly *Build* Site

Week of _____

PRIORITIES

MONDAY

TUESDAY

WEDNESDAY

THURSDAY

FRIDAY

SATURDAY

SUNDAY

THIS WEEKS GOALS

NOTES

Purpose in Action

Date: _____

6AM _____

7AM _____

8AM _____

9AM _____

10AM _____

11AM _____

1PM _____

2PM _____

3PM _____

4PM _____

5PM _____

12PM _____

6PM _____

7PM _____

8PM _____

PRIORITIES

☐

☐

☐

☐

☐

☐

☐

☐

☐

NOTES

Purpose in Action

Date: _____

Time	
6AM	
7AM	
8AM	
9AM	
10AM	
11AM	
1PM	
2PM	
3PM	
4PM	
5PM	
12PM	
6PM	
7PM	
8PM	

PRIORITIES

☐
☐
☐
☐
☐
☐
☐
☐
☐

NOTES

Purpose in Action

Date: _____

6AM _____

7AM _____

8AM _____

9AM _____

10AM _____

11AM _____

1PM _____

2PM _____

3PM _____

4PM _____

5PM _____

12PM _____

6PM _____

7PM _____

8PM _____

PRIORITIES

☐

☐

☐

☐

☐

☐

☐

☐

☐

NOTES

Purpose in Action

Date: _____

6AM _____

7AM _____

8AM _____

9AM _____

10AM _____

11AM _____

1PM _____

2PM _____

3PM _____

4PM _____

5PM _____

12PM _____

6PM _____

7PM _____

8PM _____

PRIORITIES

☐

☐

☐

☐

☐

☐

☐

☐

☐

NOTES

Date: _____

6AM _____

7AM _____

8AM _____

9AM _____

10AM _____

11AM _____

1PM _____

2PM _____

3PM _____

4PM _____

5PM _____

12PM _____

6PM _____

7PM _____

8PM _____

PRIORITIES

☐

☐

☐

☐

☐

☐

☐

☐

☐

NOTES

Purpose in Action

Date: _____

6AM _____

7AM _____

8AM _____

9AM _____

10AM _____

11AM _____

1PM _____

2PM _____

3PM _____

4PM _____

5PM _____

12PM _____

6PM _____

7PM _____

8PM _____

PRIORITIES

- ☐
- ☐
- ☐
- ☐
- ☐
- ☐
- ☐
- ☐
- ☐

NOTES

Date: _____

6AM _____

7AM _____

8AM _____

9AM _____

10AM _____

11AM _____

1PM _____

2PM _____

3PM _____

4PM _____

5PM _____

12PM _____

6PM _____

7PM _____

8PM _____

PRIORITIES

☐
☐
☐
☐
☐
☐
☐
☐
☐

NOTES

Weekly Site Check

• •

• This week, I'm most proud of:

_____

• One habit or action that moved me closer to purpose:

_____

• One thing I need to shift or improve next week:

_____

• What I learned about myself:

_____

• How I honored my peace this week:

☐ Rested intentionally

☐ Set boundaries

☐ Spoke kindly to myself

☐ Asked for support

☐ Stayed off social when needed

☐ Other: _____

Mantra / Scripture / Affirmation I'm carrying into next week:

_____

Weekly Build Site

· ·

Week of _____

PRIORITIES

MONDAY

TUESDAY

WEDNESDAY

THURSDAY

FRIDAY

SATURDAY

SUNDAY

THIS WEEKS GOALS

NOTES

Purpose in Action

Date: _____

6AM _____

7AM _____

8AM _____

9AM _____

10AM _____

11AM _____

1PM _____

2PM _____

3PM _____

4PM _____

5PM _____

12PM _____

6PM _____

7PM _____

8PM _____

PRIORITIES

- ☐
- ☐
- ☐
- ☐
- ☐
- ☐
- ☐
- ☐
- ☐

NOTES

Purpose in Action

Date: _____

6AM _____

7AM _____

8AM _____

9AM _____

10AM _____

11AM _____

1PM _____

2PM _____

3PM _____

4PM _____

5PM _____

12PM _____

6PM _____

7PM _____

8PM _____

PRIORITIES

☐

☐

☐

☐

☐

☐

☐

☐

☐

NOTES

Purpose in Action

Date: _____

6AM _____

7AM _____

8AM _____

9AM _____

10AM _____

11AM _____

1PM _____

2PM _____

3PM _____

4PM _____

5PM _____

12PM _____

6PM _____

7PM _____

8PM _____

PRIORITIES

☐

☐

☐

☐

☐

☐

☐

☐

☐

NOTES

Purpose in Action

Date: _____

6AM _____

7AM _____

8AM _____

9AM _____

10AM _____

11AM _____

1PM _____

2PM _____

3PM _____

4PM _____

5PM _____

12PM _____

6PM _____

7PM _____

8PM _____

PRIORITIES

☐

☐

☐

☐

☐

☐

☐

☐

☐

NOTES

Purpose in Action

Date: _____

6AM _____

7AM _____

8AM _____

9AM _____

10AM _____

11AM _____

1PM _____

2PM _____

3PM _____

4PM _____

5PM _____

12PM _____

6PM _____

7PM _____

8PM _____

PRIORITIES

☐
☐
☐
☐
☐
☐
☐
☐
☐

NOTES

Purpose in Action

Date: _____

6AM _____

7AM _____

8AM _____

9AM _____

10AM _____

11AM _____

1PM _____

2PM _____

3PM _____

4PM _____

5PM _____

12PM _____

6PM _____

7PM _____

8PM _____

PRIORITIES

☐

☐

☐

☐

☐

☐

☐

☐

☐

NOTES

Date: _____

6AM _____

7AM _____

8AM _____

9AM _____

10AM _____

11AM _____

1PM _____

2PM _____

3PM _____

4PM _____

5PM _____

12PM _____

6PM _____

7PM _____

8PM _____

PRIORITIES

☐

☐

☐

☐

☐

☐

☐

☐

☐

NOTES

Weekly Site Check

• •

• This week, I'm most proud of:

_____

• One habit or action that moved me closer to purpose:

_____

• One thing I need to shift or improve next week:

_____

• What I learned about myself:

_____

• How I honored my peace this week:

☐ Rested intentionally

☐ Set boundaries

☐ Spoke kindly to myself

☐ Asked for support

☐ Stayed off social when needed

☐ Other: _____

Mantra / Scripture / Affirmation I'm carrying into next week:

_____

Weekly *Build* Site

· ·

Week of _____

PRIORITIES

MONDAY

TUESDAY

WEDNESDAY

THURSDAY

FRIDAY

SATURDAY

SUNDAY

THIS WEEKS GOALS

NOTES

Purpose in Action

Date: _____

6AM _____

7AM _____

8AM _____

9AM _____

10AM _____

11AM _____

1PM _____

2PM _____

3PM _____

4PM _____

5PM _____

12PM _____

6PM _____

7PM _____

8PM _____

PRIORITIES

- ☐
- ☐
- ☐
- ☐
- ☐
- ☐
- ☐
- ☐
- ☐

NOTES

Purpose in Action

Date: _____

Time	
6AM	_____
7AM	_____
8AM	_____
9AM	_____
10AM	_____
11AM	_____
1PM	_____
2PM	_____
3PM	_____
4PM	_____
5PM	_____
12PM	_____
6PM	_____
7PM	_____
8PM	_____

PRIORITIES

- ☐
- ☐
- ☐
- ☐
- ☐
- ☐
- ☐
- ☐
- ☐

NOTES

Purpose in Action

Date: _____

6AM _____

7AM _____

8AM _____

9AM _____

10AM _____

11AM _____

1PM _____

2PM _____

3PM _____

4PM _____

5PM _____

12PM _____

6PM _____

7PM _____

8PM _____

PRIORITIES

- ☐
- ☐
- ☐
- ☐
- ☐
- ☐
- ☐
- ☐
- ☐

NOTES

Purpose in Action

Date: _____

6AM _____

7AM _____

8AM _____

9AM _____

10AM _____

11AM _____

1PM _____

2PM _____

3PM _____

4PM _____

5PM _____

12PM _____

6PM _____

7PM _____

8PM _____

PRIORITIES

☐

☐

☐

☐

☐

☐

☐

☐

☐

NOTES

Date: _____

6AM _____

7AM _____

8AM _____

9AM _____

10AM _____

11AM _____

1PM _____

2PM _____

3PM _____

4PM _____

5PM _____

12PM _____

6PM _____

7PM _____

8PM _____

PRIORITIES

☐

☐

☐

☐

☐

☐

☐

☐

☐

NOTES

Purpose in Action

Date: _____

6AM _____

7AM _____

8AM _____

9AM _____

10AM _____

11AM _____

1PM _____

2PM _____

3PM _____

4PM _____

5PM _____

12PM _____

6PM _____

7PM _____

8PM _____

PRIORITIES

☐
☐
☐
☐
☐
☐
☐
☐
☐

NOTES

Purpose in Action

Date: _____

6AM _____

7AM _____

8AM _____

9AM _____

10AM _____

11AM _____

1PM _____

2PM _____

3PM _____

4PM _____

5PM _____

12PM _____

6PM _____

7PM _____

8PM _____

PRIORITIES

☐

☐

☐

☐

☐

☐

☐

☐

☐

NOTES

Weekly Site Check

• •

• This week, I'm most proud of:

_____

• One habit or action that moved me closer to purpose:

_____

• One thing I need to shift or improve next week:

_____

• What I learned about myself:

_____

• How I honored my peace this week:

☐ Rested intentionally

☐ Set boundaries

☐ Spoke kindly to myself

☐ Asked for support

☐ Stayed off social when needed

☐ Other: _____

Mantra / Scripture / Affirmation I'm carrying into next week:

_____

Weekly *Build* Site

· ·

Week of _____

PRIORITIES

MONDAY

TUESDAY

WEDNESDAY

THURSDAY

FRIDAY

SATURDAY

SUNDAY

THIS WEEKS GOALS

NOTES

Purpose in Action

Date: _____

6AM _____

7AM _____

8AM _____

9AM _____

10AM _____

11AM _____

1PM _____

2PM _____

3PM _____

4PM _____

5PM _____

12PM _____

6PM _____

7PM _____

8PM _____

PRIORITIES

☐

☐

☐

☐

☐

☐

☐

☐

☐

NOTES

Purpose in Action

Date: _____

6AM _____

7AM _____

8AM _____

9AM _____

10AM _____

11AM _____

1PM _____

2PM _____

3PM _____

4PM _____

5PM _____

12PM _____

6PM _____

7PM _____

8PM _____

PRIORITIES

☐
☐
☐
☐
☐
☐
☐
☐
☐

NOTES

Purpose in Action

Date: _____

6AM _____

7AM _____

8AM _____

9AM _____

10AM _____

11AM _____

1PM _____

2PM _____

3PM _____

4PM _____

5PM _____

12PM _____

6PM _____

7PM _____

8PM _____

PRIORITIES

☐

☐

☐

☐

☐

☐

☐

☐

☐

NOTES

Purpose in Action

Date: _____

6AM _____

7AM _____

8AM _____

9AM _____

10AM _____

11AM _____

1PM _____

2PM _____

3PM _____

4PM _____

5PM _____

12PM _____

6PM _____

7PM _____

8PM _____

PRIORITIES

☐

☐

☐

☐

☐

☐

☐

☐

☐

NOTES

Date: _____

	PRIORITIES

6AM _____

☐

7AM _____

☐

8AM _____

☐

9AM _____

☐

10AM _____

☐

11AM _____

☐

1PM _____

☐

2PM _____

☐

NOTES

3PM _____

4PM _____

5PM _____

12PM _____

6PM _____

7PM _____

8PM _____

Purpose in Action

Date: _____

6AM _____

7AM _____

8AM _____

9AM _____

10AM _____

11AM _____

1PM _____

2PM _____

3PM _____

4PM _____

5PM _____

12PM _____

6PM _____

7PM _____

8PM _____

PRIORITIES

☐

☐

☐

☐

☐

☐

☐

☐

☐

NOTES

Purpose in Action

Date: _____

Time	
6AM	
7AM	
8AM	
9AM	
10AM	
11AM	
1PM	
2PM	
3PM	
4PM	
5PM	
12PM	
6PM	
7PM	
8PM	

PRIORITIES

☐
☐
☐
☐
☐
☐
☐
☐
☐

NOTES

Weekly Site Check

• •

• This week, I'm most proud of:

_____

• One habit or action that moved me closer to purpose:

_____

• One thing I need to shift or improve next week:

_____

• What I learned about myself:

_____

• How I honored my peace this week:

☐ Rested intentionally

☐ Set boundaries

☐ Spoke kindly to myself

☐ Asked for support

☐ Stayed off social when needed

☐ Other: _____

Mantra / Scripture / Affirmation I'm carrying into next week:

_____

Progress Report

· ·

Check in with the progress you've made so far.

What goals have you *crushed?*
Which ones are still unfolding?
Which ones need to be paused or reworked?

Use this page to **course-correct with clarity** — not judgment. Progress is a process, and every win (big or small) counts.

Goals Accomplished ✅

Goals Still in Progress 🔄

Goals on Pause ⏸

Lessons Learned (Grows)

WHAT I'M CELEBRATING

Add Month

_____

Notes	SUNDAY	MONDAY	TUESDAY
	☐	☐	☐
	☐	☐	☐
	☐	☐	☐
	☐	☐	☐
	☐	☐	☐

Add Year

_____

WEDNESDAY	THURSDAY	FRIDAY	SATURDAY
☐	☐	☐	☐
☐	☐	☐	☐
☐	☐	☐	☐
☐	☐	☐	☐
☐	☐	☐	☐

Weekly Build Site

Week of _____

MONDAY

TUESDAY

WEDNESDAY

THURSDAY

FRIDAY

SATURDAY

SUNDAY

THIS WEEKS GOALS

NOTES

Purpose in Action

Date: _____

6AM _____

7AM _____

8AM _____

9AM _____

10AM _____

11AM _____

1PM _____

2PM _____

3PM _____

4PM _____

5PM _____

12PM _____

6PM _____

7PM _____

8PM _____

PRIORITIES

☐

☐

☐

☐

☐

☐

☐

☐

☐

NOTES

Purpose in Action

Date: _____

6AM _____

7AM _____

8AM _____

9AM _____

10AM _____

11AM _____

1PM _____

2PM _____

3PM _____

4PM _____

5PM _____

12PM _____

6PM _____

7PM _____

8PM _____

PRIORITIES

☐

☐

☐

☐

☐

☐

☐

☐

☐

NOTES

Purpose in Action

Date: _____

6AM _____

7AM _____

8AM _____

9AM _____

10AM _____

11AM _____

1PM _____

2PM _____

3PM _____

4PM _____

5PM _____

12PM _____

6PM _____

7PM _____

8PM _____

PRIORITIES

- [ ]
- [ ]
- [ ]
- [ ]
- [ ]
- [ ]
- [ ]
- [ ]
- [ ]

NOTES

Purpose in Action

Date: _____

6AM _____

7AM _____

8AM _____

9AM _____

10AM _____

11AM _____

1PM _____

2PM _____

3PM _____

4PM _____

5PM _____

12PM _____

6PM _____

7PM _____

8PM _____

PRIORITIES

- ☐
- ☐
- ☐
- ☐
- ☐
- ☐
- ☐
- ☐
- ☐

NOTES

Purpose in Action

Date: _____

6AM _____

7AM _____

8AM _____

9AM _____

10AM _____

11AM _____

1PM _____

2PM _____

3PM _____

4PM _____

5PM _____

12PM _____

6PM _____

7PM _____

8PM _____

PRIORITIES

☐

☐

☐

☐

☐

☐

☐

☐

☐

NOTES

Purpose in Action

Date: _____

6AM _____

7AM _____

8AM _____

9AM _____

10AM _____

11AM _____

1PM _____

2PM _____

3PM _____

4PM _____

5PM _____

12PM _____

6PM _____

7PM _____

8PM _____

PRIORITIES

☐
☐
☐
☐
☐
☐
☐
☐
☐

NOTES

Date: _____

6AM _____

7AM _____

8AM _____

9AM _____

10AM _____

11AM _____

1PM _____

2PM _____

3PM _____

4PM _____

5PM _____

12PM _____

6PM _____

7PM _____

8PM _____

PRIORITIES

- [ ]
- [ ]
- [ ]
- [ ]
- [ ]
- [ ]
- [ ]
- [ ]
- [ ]

NOTES

Weekly Site Check

• This week, I'm most proud of:

_____

• One habit or action that moved me closer to purpose:

_____

• One thing I need to shift or improve next week:

_____

• What I learned about myself:

_____

• How I honored my peace this week:

☐ Rested intentionally

☐ Set boundaries

☐ Spoke kindly to myself

☐ Asked for support

☐ Stayed off social when needed

☐ Other: _____

Mantra / Scripture / Affirmation I'm carrying into next week:

_____

Weekly *Build* Site

• •

Week of _____

PRIORITIES

MONDAY

TUESDAY

WEDNESDAY

THURSDAY

FRIDAY

SATURDAY

SUNDAY

THIS WEEKS GOALS

NOTES

Date: _____

6AM _____

7AM _____

8AM _____

9AM _____

10AM _____

11AM _____

1PM _____

2PM _____

3PM _____

4PM _____

5PM _____

12PM _____

6PM _____

7PM _____

8PM _____

PRIORITIES

☐

☐

☐

☐

☐

☐

☐

☐

☐

NOTES

Purpose in Action

Date: _____

6AM _____

7AM _____

8AM _____

9AM _____

10AM _____

11AM _____

1PM _____

2PM _____

3PM _____

4PM _____

5PM _____

12PM _____

6PM _____

7PM _____

8PM _____

PRIORITIES

☐

☐

☐

☐

☐

☐

☐

☐

☐

NOTES

Purpose in Action

Date: _____

6AM _____

7AM _____

8AM _____

9AM _____

10AM _____

11AM _____

1PM _____

2PM _____

3PM _____

4PM _____

5PM _____

12PM _____

6PM _____

7PM _____

8PM _____

PRIORITIES

☐
☐
☐
☐
☐
☐
☐
☐
☐

NOTES

Purpose in Action

Date: _____

6AM _____	
7AM _____	
8AM _____	
9AM _____	
10AM _____	
11AM _____	
1PM _____	
2PM _____	
3PM _____	
4PM _____	
5PM _____	
12PM _____	
6PM _____	
7PM _____	
8PM _____	

PRIORITIES

☐
☐
☐
☐
☐
☐
☐
☐
☐

NOTES

Date: _____

6AM _____

7AM _____

8AM _____

9AM _____

10AM _____

11AM _____

1PM _____

2PM _____

3PM _____

4PM _____

5PM _____

12PM _____

6PM _____

7PM _____

8PM _____

PRIORITIES

- ☐
- ☐
- ☐
- ☐
- ☐
- ☐
- ☐
- ☐
- ☐

NOTES

Purpose in Action

Date: _____

6AM _____

7AM _____

8AM _____

9AM _____

10AM _____

11AM _____

1PM _____

2PM _____

3PM _____

4PM _____

5PM _____

12PM _____

6PM _____

7PM _____

8PM _____

PRIORITIES

☐
☐
☐
☐
☐
☐
☐
☐
☐

NOTES

Date: _____

6AM _____

7AM _____

8AM _____

9AM _____

10AM _____

11AM _____

1PM _____

2PM _____

3PM _____

4PM _____

5PM _____

12PM _____

6PM _____

7PM _____

8PM _____

PRIORITIES

- [ ]
- [ ]
- [ ]
- [ ]
- [ ]
- [ ]
- [ ]
- [ ]
- [ ]

NOTES

Weekly Site Check

• •

• This week, I'm most proud of:

_____

• One habit or action that moved me closer to purpose:

_____

• One thing I need to shift or improve next week:

_____

• What I learned about myself:

_____

• How I honored my peace this week:

☐ Rested intentionally

☐ Set boundaries

☐ Spoke kindly to myself

☐ Asked for support

☐ Stayed off social when needed

☐ Other: _____

Mantra / Scripture / Affirmation I'm carrying into next week:

_____

Weekly *Build* Site

· ·

Week of _____

PRIORITIES

MONDAY	THIS WEEKS GOALS
TUESDAY	
WEDNESDAY	
THURSDAY	
FRIDAY	NOTES
SATURDAY	
SUNDAY	

Purpose in Action

Date: _____

6AM _____

7AM _____

8AM _____

9AM _____

10AM _____

11AM _____

1PM _____

2PM _____

3PM _____

4PM _____

5PM _____

12PM _____

6PM _____

7PM _____

8PM _____

PRIORITIES

☐

☐

☐

☐

☐

☐

☐

☐

☐

NOTES

Purpose in Action

Date: _____

6AM _____

7AM _____

8AM _____

9AM _____

10AM _____

11AM _____

1PM _____

2PM _____

3PM _____

4PM _____

5PM _____

12PM _____

6PM _____

7PM _____

8PM _____

PRIORITIES

☐

☐

☐

☐

☐

☐

☐

☐

☐

NOTES

Purpose in Action

Date: _____

6AM _____	

PRIORITIES

- ☐
- ☐
- ☐
- ☐
- ☐
- ☐
- ☐
- ☐
- ☐

6AM _____

7AM _____

8AM _____

9AM _____

10AM _____

11AM _____

1PM _____

2PM _____

3PM _____

4PM _____

5PM _____

12PM _____

6PM _____

7PM _____

8PM _____

NOTES

Purpose in Action

Date: _____

6AM _____

7AM _____

8AM _____

9AM _____

10AM _____

11AM _____

1PM _____

2PM _____

3PM _____

4PM _____

5PM _____

12PM _____

6PM _____

7PM _____

8PM _____

PRIORITIES

☐
☐
☐
☐
☐
☐
☐
☐
☐

NOTES

Purpose in Action

Date: _____

6AM _____

7AM _____

8AM _____

9AM _____

10AM _____

11AM _____

1PM _____

2PM _____

3PM _____

4PM _____

5PM _____

12PM _____

6PM _____

7PM _____

8PM _____

PRIORITIES

- ☐
- ☐
- ☐
- ☐
- ☐
- ☐
- ☐
- ☐
- ☐

NOTES

Purpose in Action

Date: _____

6AM _____

7AM _____

8AM _____

9AM _____

10AM _____

11AM _____

1PM _____

2PM _____

3PM _____

4PM _____

5PM _____

12PM _____

6PM _____

7PM _____

8PM _____

PRIORITIES

☐

☐

☐

☐

☐

☐

☐

☐

☐

NOTES

Purpose in Action

Date: _____

6AM _____

7AM _____

8AM _____

9AM _____

10AM _____

11AM _____

1PM _____

2PM _____

3PM _____

4PM _____

5PM _____

12PM _____

6PM _____

7PM _____

8PM _____

PRIORITIES

- [ ]
- [ ]
- [ ]
- [ ]
- [ ]
- [ ]
- [ ]
- [ ]
- [ ]

NOTES

Weekly Site Check

• •

• This week, I'm most proud of:

_____

• One habit or action that moved me closer to purpose:

_____

• One thing I need to shift or improve next week:

_____

• What I learned about myself:

_____

• How I honored my peace this week:

☐ Rested intentionally

☐ Set boundaries

☐ Spoke kindly to myself

☐ Asked for support

☐ Stayed off social when needed

☐ Other: _____

Mantra / Scripture / Affirmation I'm carrying into next week:

_____

"She remembered who she was and the game changed."

- Lalah Delia

Weekly *Build* Site

· ·

Week of _____

PRIORITIES

MONDAY

TUESDAY

WEDNESDAY

THURSDAY

FRIDAY

SATURDAY

SUNDAY

THIS WEEKS GOALS

NOTES

Purpose in Action

Date: _____

6AM _____

7AM _____

8AM _____

9AM _____

10AM _____

11AM _____

1PM _____

2PM _____

3PM _____

4PM _____

5PM _____

12PM _____

6PM _____

7PM _____

8PM _____

PRIORITIES

☐

☐

☐

☐

☐

☐

☐

☐

☐

NOTES

Purpose in Action

Date: _____

6AM _____

7AM _____

8AM _____

9AM _____

10AM _____

11AM _____

1PM _____

2PM _____

3PM _____

4PM _____

5PM _____

12PM _____

6PM _____

7PM _____

8PM _____

PRIORITIES

☐
☐
☐
☐
☐
☐
☐
☐
☐

NOTES

Date: _____

6AM _____

7AM _____

8AM _____

9AM _____

10AM _____

11AM _____

1PM _____

2PM _____

3PM _____

4PM _____

5PM _____

12PM _____

6PM _____

7PM _____

8PM _____

PRIORITIES

☐

☐

☐

☐

☐

☐

☐

☐

☐

NOTES

Purpose in Action

Date: _____

6AM _____

7AM _____

8AM _____

9AM _____

10AM _____

11AM _____

1PM _____

2PM _____

3PM _____

4PM _____

5PM _____

12PM _____

6PM _____

7PM _____

8PM _____

PRIORITIES

☐

☐

☐

☐

☐

☐

☐

☐

☐

NOTES

Date: _____

6AM _____

7AM _____

8AM _____

9AM _____

10AM _____

11AM _____

1PM _____

2PM _____

3PM _____

4PM _____

5PM _____

12PM _____

6PM _____

7PM _____

8PM _____

PRIORITIES

☐

☐

☐

☐

☐

☐

☐

☐

☐

NOTES

Purpose in Action

Date: _____

6AM _____

7AM _____

8AM _____

9AM _____

10AM _____

11AM _____

1PM _____

2PM _____

3PM _____

4PM _____

5PM _____

12PM _____

6PM _____

7PM _____

8PM _____

PRIORITIES

☐

☐

☐

☐

☐

☐

☐

☐

☐

NOTES

Purpose in Action

Date: _____

6AM _____

7AM _____

8AM _____

9AM _____

10AM _____

11AM _____

1PM _____

2PM _____

3PM _____

4PM _____

5PM _____

12PM _____

6PM _____

7PM _____

8PM _____

PRIORITIES

☐

☐

☐

☐

☐

☐

☐

☐

☐

NOTES

Weekly Site Check

• •

• This week, I'm most proud of:

_____

• One habit or action that moved me closer to purpose:

_____

• One thing I need to shift or improve next week:

_____

• What I learned about myself:

_____

• How I honored my peace this week:

☐ Rested intentionally

☐ Set boundaries

☐ Spoke kindly to myself

☐ Asked for support

☐ Stayed off social when needed

☐ Other: _____

Mantra / Scripture / Affirmation I'm carrying into next week:

_____

Progress Report

Check in with the progress you've made so far.

What goals have you *crushed?*
Which ones are still unfolding?
Which ones need to be paused or reworked?

Use this page to **course-correct with clarity** — not judgment. Progress is a process, and every win (big or small) counts.

Goals Accomplished ✅

Goals Still in Progress 🔄

Goals on Pause ⏸

Lessons Learned (Grows)

WHAT I'M CELEBRATING

Add Month

_____

Notes	SUNDAY	MONDAY	TUESDAY
	☐	☐	☐
	☐	☐	☐
	☐	☐	☐
	☐	☐	☐
	☐	☐	☐

Add Year

_____

WEDNESDAY	THURSDAY	FRIDAY	SATURDAY
☐	☐	☐	☐
☐	☐	☐	☐
☐	☐	☐	☐
☐	☐	☐	☐
☐	☐	☐	☐

Weekly Build Site

Week of _____

PRIORITIES

MONDAY

TUESDAY

WEDNESDAY

THURSDAY

FRIDAY

SATURDAY

SUNDAY

THIS WEEKS GOALS

NOTES

Purpose in Action

Date: _____

6AM _____

7AM _____

8AM _____

9AM _____

10AM _____

11AM _____

1PM _____

2PM _____

3PM _____

4PM _____

5PM _____

12PM _____

6PM _____

7PM _____

8PM _____

PRIORITIES

☐

☐

☐

☐

☐

☐

☐

☐

☐

NOTES

Purpose in Action

Date: _____

Time	
6AM	_____
7AM	_____
8AM	_____
9AM	_____
10AM	_____
11AM	_____
1PM	_____
2PM	_____
3PM	_____
4PM	_____
5PM	_____
12PM	_____
6PM	_____
7PM	_____
8PM	_____

PRIORITIES

- ☐
- ☐
- ☐
- ☐
- ☐
- ☐
- ☐
- ☐
- ☐

NOTES

Purpose in Action

Date: _____

6AM _____	**PRIORITIES**
7AM _____	☐
8AM _____	☐
9AM _____	☐
10AM _____	☐
11AM _____	☐
1PM _____	☐
	☐
	☐

6AM _____

7AM _____

8AM _____

9AM _____

10AM _____

11AM _____

1PM _____

2PM _____

3PM _____

4PM _____

5PM _____

12PM _____

6PM _____

7PM _____

8PM _____

PRIORITIES

☐
☐
☐
☐
☐
☐
☐
☐
☐

NOTES

Purpose in Action

Date: _____

6AM _____

7AM _____

8AM _____

9AM _____

10AM _____

11AM _____

1PM _____

2PM _____

3PM _____

4PM _____

5PM _____

12PM _____

6PM _____

7PM _____

8PM _____

PRIORITIES

☐

☐

☐

☐

☐

☐

☐

☐

☐

NOTES

Purpose in Action

Date: _____

6AM _____

7AM _____

8AM _____

9AM _____

10AM _____

11AM _____

1PM _____

2PM _____

3PM _____

4PM _____

5PM _____

12PM _____

6PM _____

7PM _____

8PM _____

PRIORITIES

- ☐
- ☐
- ☐
- ☐
- ☐
- ☐
- ☐
- ☐
- ☐

NOTES

Purpose in Action

Date: _____

6AM _____

7AM _____

8AM _____

9AM _____

10AM _____

11AM _____

1PM _____

2PM _____

3PM _____

4PM _____

5PM _____

12PM _____

6PM _____

7PM _____

8PM _____

PRIORITIES

☐

☐

☐

☐

☐

☐

☐

☐

☐

NOTES

Purpose in Action

Date: _____

6AM _____	**PRIORITIES**
7AM _____	☐
8AM _____	☐
9AM _____	☐
10AM _____	☐
11AM _____	☐
1PM _____	☐
2PM _____	☐
3PM _____	☐
4PM _____	
5PM _____	**NOTES**
12PM _____	
6PM _____	
7PM _____	
8PM _____	

SHE REFLECTS:

Weekly *Site* Check

• •

- This week, I'm most proud of:

  _____

- One habit or action that moved me closer to purpose:

  _____

- One thing I need to shift or improve next week:

  _____

- What I learned about myself:

  _____

- How I honored my peace this week:

  ☐ Rested intentionally

  ☐ Set boundaries

  ☐ Spoke kindly to myself

  ☐ Asked for support

  ☐ Stayed off social when needed

  ☐ Other: _____

Mantra / Scripture / Affirmation I'm carrying into next week:

  _____

"Discipline is choosing between what you want now and what you want most."

- Abraham Lincoln

Weekly *Build* Site

• •

Week of _____

PRIORITIES

MONDAY

TUESDAY

WEDNESDAY

THURSDAY

FRIDAY

SATURDAY

SUNDAY

THIS WEEKS GOALS

NOTES

Purpose in Action

Date: _____

6AM _____

7AM _____

8AM _____

9AM _____

10AM _____

11AM _____

1PM _____

2PM _____

3PM _____

4PM _____

5PM _____

12PM _____

6PM _____

7PM _____

8PM _____

PRIORITIES

☐

☐

☐

☐

☐

☐

☐

☐

☐

NOTES

Purpose in Action

Date: _____

6AM _____

7AM _____

8AM _____

9AM _____

10AM _____

11AM _____

1PM _____

2PM _____

3PM _____

4PM _____

5PM _____

12PM _____

6PM _____

7PM _____

8PM _____

PRIORITIES

☐

☐

☐

☐

☐

☐

☐

☐

☐

NOTES

Purpose in Action

Date: _____

6AM _____

7AM _____

8AM _____

9AM _____

10AM _____

11AM _____

1PM _____

2PM _____

3PM _____

4PM _____

5PM _____

12PM _____

6PM _____

7PM _____

8PM _____

PRIORITIES

- ☐
- ☐
- ☐
- ☐
- ☐
- ☐
- ☐
- ☐
- ☐

NOTES

Purpose in Action

Date: _____

6AM _____

7AM _____

8AM _____

9AM _____

10AM _____

11AM _____

1PM _____

2PM _____

3PM _____

4PM _____

5PM _____

12PM _____

6PM _____

7PM _____

8PM _____

PRIORITIES

☐

☐

☐

☐

☐

☐

☐

☐

☐

NOTES

Purpose in Action

Date: _____

6AM _____

7AM _____

8AM _____

9AM _____

10AM _____

11AM _____

1PM _____

2PM _____

3PM _____

4PM _____

5PM _____

12PM _____

6PM _____

7PM _____

8PM _____

PRIORITIES

☐
☐
☐
☐
☐
☐
☐
☐
☐

NOTES

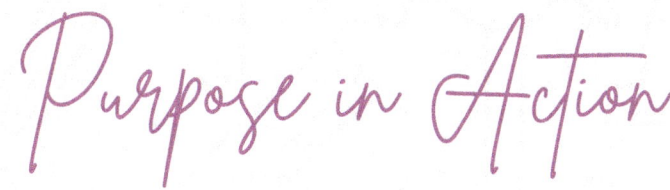

Purpose in Action

Date: _____

6AM _____

7AM _____

8AM _____

9AM _____

10AM _____

11AM _____

1PM _____

2PM _____

3PM _____

4PM _____

5PM _____

12PM _____

6PM _____

7PM _____

8PM _____

PRIORITIES

☐

☐

☐

☐

☐

☐

☐

☐

☐

NOTES

Purpose in Action

Date: _____

6AM _____

7AM _____

8AM _____

9AM _____

10AM _____

11AM _____

1PM _____

2PM _____

3PM _____

4PM _____

5PM _____

12PM _____

6PM _____

7PM _____

8PM _____

PRIORITIES

☐

☐

☐

☐

☐

☐

☐

☐

☐

NOTES

SHE REFLECTS:

Weekly *Site* Check

• •

• This week, I'm most proud of:

_____

• One habit or action that moved me closer to purpose:

_____

• One thing I need to shift or improve next week:

_____

• What I learned about myself:

_____

• How I honored my peace this week:

☐ Rested intentionally

☐ Set boundaries

☐ Spoke kindly to myself

☐ Asked for support

☐ Stayed off social when needed

☐ Other: _____

Mantra / Scripture / Affirmation I'm carrying into next week:

_____

Weekly *Build* Site

· ·

Week of _____

PRIORITIES

MONDAY

TUESDAY

WEDNESDAY

THURSDAY

FRIDAY

SATURDAY

SUNDAY

THIS WEEKS GOALS

NOTES

Purpose in Action

Date: _____

Time	
6AM	_____
7AM	_____
8AM	_____
9AM	_____
10AM	_____
11AM	_____
1PM	_____
2PM	_____
3PM	_____
4PM	_____
5PM	_____
12PM	_____
6PM	_____
7PM	_____
8PM	_____

PRIORITIES

☐
☐
☐
☐
☐
☐
☐
☐
☐

NOTES

Date: _____

6AM _____

7AM _____

8AM _____

9AM _____

10AM _____

11AM _____

1PM _____

2PM _____

3PM _____

4PM _____

5PM _____

12PM _____

6PM _____

7PM _____

8PM _____

PRIORITIES

- ☐
- ☐
- ☐
- ☐
- ☐
- ☐
- ☐
- ☐
- ☐

NOTES

Purpose in Action

Date: _____

6AM _____

7AM _____

8AM _____

9AM _____

10AM _____

11AM _____

1PM _____

2PM _____

3PM _____

4PM _____

5PM _____

12PM _____

6PM _____

7PM _____

8PM _____

PRIORITIES

☐
☐
☐
☐
☐
☐
☐
☐
☐

NOTES

Date: _____

6AM _____

7AM _____

8AM _____

9AM _____

10AM _____

11AM _____

1PM _____

2PM _____

3PM _____

4PM _____

5PM _____

12PM _____

6PM _____

7PM _____

8PM _____

PRIORITIES

☐

☐

☐

☐

☐

☐

☐

☐

☐

NOTES

Purpose in Action

Date: _____

6AM _____

7AM _____

8AM _____

9AM _____

10AM _____

11AM _____

1PM _____

2PM _____

3PM _____

4PM _____

5PM _____

12PM _____

6PM _____

7PM _____

8PM _____

PRIORITIES

☐

☐

☐

☐

☐

☐

☐

☐

☐

NOTES

Purpose in Action

Date: _____

6AM _____

7AM _____

8AM _____

9AM _____

10AM _____

11AM _____

1PM _____

2PM _____

3PM _____

4PM _____

5PM _____

12PM _____

6PM _____

7PM _____

8PM _____

PRIORITIES

☐

☐

☐

☐

☐

☐

☐

☐

☐

NOTES

Purpose in Action

Date: _____

6AM _____

7AM _____

8AM _____

9AM _____

10AM _____

11AM _____

1PM _____

2PM _____

3PM _____

4PM _____

5PM _____

12PM _____

6PM _____

7PM _____

8PM _____

PRIORITIES

☐
☐
☐
☐
☐
☐
☐
☐
☐

NOTES

Weekly Site Check

• •

• This week, I'm most proud of:

_____

• One habit or action that moved me closer to purpose:

_____

• One thing I need to shift or improve next week:

_____

• What I learned about myself:

_____

• How I honored my peace this week:

☐ Rested intentionally

☐ Set boundaries

☐ Spoke kindly to myself

☐ Asked for support

☐ Stayed off social when needed

☐ Other: _____

Mantra / Scripture / Affirmation I'm carrying into next week:

_____

"God is within her, she will not fall."

- Psalm 46:5

Weekly Build Site

Week of _____

PRIORITIES

MONDAY	THIS WEEKS GOALS
TUESDAY	
WEDNESDAY	
THURSDAY	
FRIDAY	NOTES
SATURDAY	
SUNDAY	

Purpose in Action

Date: _____

6AM _____

7AM _____

8AM _____

9AM _____

10AM _____

11AM _____

1PM _____

2PM _____

3PM _____

4PM _____

5PM _____

12PM _____

6PM _____

7PM _____

8PM _____

PRIORITIES

☐
☐
☐
☐
☐
☐
☐
☐
☐

NOTES

Purpose in Action

Date: _____

6AM _____

7AM _____

8AM _____

9AM _____

10AM _____

11AM _____

1PM _____

2PM _____

3PM _____

4PM _____

5PM _____

12PM _____

6PM _____

7PM _____

8PM _____

PRIORITIES

☐

☐

☐

☐

☐

☐

☐

☐

☐

NOTES

Purpose in Action

Date: _____

6AM _____

7AM _____

8AM _____

9AM _____

10AM _____

11AM _____

1PM _____

2PM _____

3PM _____

4PM _____

5PM _____

12PM _____

6PM _____

7PM _____

8PM _____

PRIORITIES

☐

☐

☐

☐

☐

☐

☐

☐

☐

NOTES

Date: _____

6AM _____

7AM _____

8AM _____

9AM _____

10AM _____

11AM _____

1PM _____

2PM _____

3PM _____

4PM _____

5PM _____

12PM _____

6PM _____

7PM _____

8PM _____

PRIORITIES

☐

☐

☐

☐

☐

☐

☐

☐

☐

NOTES

Purpose in Action

Date: _____

6AM _____

7AM _____

8AM _____

9AM _____

10AM _____

11AM _____

1PM _____

2PM _____

3PM _____

4PM _____

5PM _____

12PM _____

6PM _____

7PM _____

8PM _____

PRIORITIES

- ☐
- ☐
- ☐
- ☐
- ☐
- ☐
- ☐
- ☐
- ☐

NOTES

Date: _____

6AM _____	**PRIORITIES**
7AM _____	☐
8AM _____	☐
9AM _____	☐
10AM _____	☐
11AM _____	☐
1PM _____	☐
2PM _____	☐
3PM _____	☐
4PM _____	
5PM _____	**NOTES**
12PM _____	
6PM _____	
7PM _____	
8PM _____	

Purpose in Action

Date: _____

6AM _____

7AM _____

8AM _____

9AM _____

10AM _____

11AM _____

1PM _____

2PM _____

3PM _____

4PM _____

5PM _____

12PM _____

6PM _____

7PM _____

8PM _____

PRIORITIES

☐

☐

☐

☐

☐

☐

☐

☐

☐

NOTES

Weekly Site Check

• •

• This week, I'm most proud of:

_____

• One habit or action that moved me closer to purpose:

_____

• One thing I need to shift or improve next week:

_____

• What I learned about myself:

_____

• How I honored my peace this week:

☐ Rested intentionally

☐ Set boundaries

☐ Spoke kindly to myself

☐ Asked for support

☐ Stayed off social when needed

☐ Other: _____

Mantra / Scripture / Affirmation I'm carrying into next week:

_____

Progress Report

Check in with the progress you've made so far.

What goals have you *crushed?*
Which ones are still unfolding?
Which ones need to be paused or reworked?

Use this page to **course-correct with clarity** — not judgment. Progress is a process, and every win (big or small) counts.

Goals Accomplished ✅

Goals Still in Progress 🔄

Goals on Pause ⏸

Lessons Learned (Grows)

WHAT I'M CELEBRATING

The *Builder's* Debrief

· ·

Take a moment to reflect on your journey over the last 90 days. What shifted? What strengthened? What surprised you? Use this space to honor your evolution. Every aligned decision, healed habit, and powerful pause added to the foundation you're building. This is your space to see yourself clearly — not just for what you've done, but for who you've become.

_____

_____

_____

_____

_____

_____

_____

- My biggest transformation: _____

- What I'm taking with me: _____

- What I'm leaving behind: _____

- My word or theme for the next season: _____

You made it.

90 days of purpose.
90 days of showing up.
90 days of choosing yourself — even when it was hard, even when it was messy, even when no one clapped.

Now pause.
Take a deep breath.
And let these words root into your spirit:

Builder's Blessing

May your hands always build what your heart believes in.
May discipline feel like devotion, not punishment.
May peace protect your pace.
May your vision stay clear, even when the path doesn't.
May what you've built in private prepare you for what's next in public.

You are she who builds — not just tasks or timelines,
but movements, legacies, and whole new realities.

Go forward bold.
Go forward grounded.
And never forget:
You are the blueprint and the builder.

Created by Dr. Dashia

Founder of *She's On Purpose*

Website: www.drdashia.com

Email: info@drdashia.com

Instagram & Facebook: @drdashia

YouTube: @shesonpurpose